UNREASONABLE
SEARCH *and* SEIZURE

THE FOURTH AMENDMENT

Hallie Murray

Enslow Publishing
101 W. 23rd Street
Suite 240
New York, NY 10011
USA

enslow.com

Published in 2018 by Enslow Publishing, LLC.
101 W. 23rd Street, Suite 240, New York, NY 10011

Library of Congress Cataloging-in-Publication Data

Names: Murray, Hallie, author.
Title: Unreasonable search and seizure : the Fourth Amendment / Hallie Murray.
Description: New York : Enslow Publishing, 2018. | Series: The Bill of Rights
  | Includes bibliographical references and index.
Identifiers: LCCN 2016057789 | ISBN 9780766085558 (library bound : alk.
paper) | ISBN 9780766087330 (paperback) | ISBN 9780766087347 (6-pack)
Subjects: LCSH: Searches and seizures—United States—Juvenile literature. |
  United States. Constitution. 4th Amendment—Juvenile literature.
Classification: LCC KF9630 .M87 2017 | DDC 3445.73/0522—dc23
LC record available at https://lccn.loc.gov/2016057789

Printed in China

To Our Readers: We have done our best to make sure all website addresses in this book were active and appropriate when we went to press. However, the author and the publisher have no control over and assume no liability for the material available on those websites or on any websites they may link to. Any comments or suggestions can be sent by e-mail to customerservice@enslow.com.

Portions of this book originally appeared in the book *The Fourth Amendment: Unreasonable Search and Seizure* by Dean Galiano.

Photo Credits: Cover, p. 1 TerryJ/E+/Getty Images; cover, interior pages (background) A-R-T/Shutterstock.com; cover, interior pages (quill) Leporska Lyubov/Shutterstock.com; p. 7 Print Collector/Hulton Archive/Getty Images; p. 10 ClassicStock/Alamy Stock Photo; p. 13 Universal Images Group/Getty Images; p. 15 © North Wind Picture Archives; p. 17 Bob Chamberlin/Los Angeles Times/Getty Images; pp. 20, 25 Bettmann/Getty Images; p. 24 Bachrach/Archive Photos/Getty Images; p. 27 Wally McNamee/Corbis/Getty Images; p. 30 New York Daily News/Getty Images; p. 34 Library of Congress; p. 37 Ute Grabowsky/Photothek/Getty Images; p. 38 Bloomberg/Getty Images; p. 41 Luke Frazza/AFP/Getty Images.

Contents

INTRODUCTION 4

CHAPTER 1

A NEW, AMERICAN GOVERNMENT........... 6

CHAPTER 2

BALANCING PRIVACY *with*
PUBLIC SAFETY 14

CHAPTER 3

THE FOURTH AMENDMENT
in the SUPREME COURT 22

CHAPTER 4

THE PROBLEM *of* NEW TECHNOLOGY..... 32

CONCLUSION.................................... 40

THE BILL OF RIGHTS......................... 43

GLOSSARY........................... 45

FURTHER READING
BOOKS *and* WEBSITES 46

BIBLIOGRAPHY...................... 47

INDEX................................ 48

INTRODUCTION

In 2013, the United States Supreme Court heard the case *Maryland v. King*, a case that was important because it helped further define the way that the American government understands the Fourth Amendment of the Constitution, the right to resist unreasonable search and seizure.

When Alonzo Jay King Jr. was arrested for first- and second-degree assault, the Maryland police took a DNA sample. This was in accordance with general police protocol in Maryland under the Maryland DNA protection act. King's DNA was matched to DNA from an unsolved rape case from 2003, and King was indicted on the basis of these results. He filed a motion to have the DNA evidence declared unusable because he said that the act of swabbing his DNA was a violation of his Fourth Amendment rights.

The Fourth Amendment states that:

> **The right of the people to be secure in their persons, houses, papers, and effects, against unreasonable searches and seizures, shall not be violated, and no Warrants shall issue, but upon probable cause, supported by Oath or affirmation, and particularly describing the place to be searched, and the persons or things to be seized.**

King said that taking the DNA amounted to an unreasonable search. However, his motion to have the DNA evidence thrown out was denied, and after a series of appeals this denial was held up in the Supreme Court.

The Supreme Court decision was very close, with only five of the nine judges in favor. These five and their supporters argued that the benefits outweighed the inconvenience and invasion of privacy involved in isolating a person's DNA after swabbing their cheek for saliva. Since cheek swabbing is a painless, medically noninvasive procedure, and since the results could help solve cold cases, it was argued that DNA testing should be allowed in such situations.

The four dissenting judges did so because they believed that according to the Fourth Amendment, governments and government services like law enforcement could not search someone for evidence of a crime without suspicion. DNA can tell scientists so much about a person that taking it seems like a big violation of privacy, but at the same time it could help keep the world safer. The Founding Fathers could not have possibly imagined the technical innovations that have been developed since the Bill of Rights was written, so it is up to the Supreme Court to decide how to interpret the amendment as it applies to new, never-before-seen situations.

CHAPTER ONE

A NEW, AMERICAN GOVERNMENT

English colonists came to America for a lot of different reasons, but many of those reasons came down to the same thing: they wanted freedom. Some, like the Puritans, had suffered religious persecution in England and wanted to begin life in a new land where they could practice their religion in peace. Others came to find economic opportunity: England at that time had a very rigid class system, and a person who was born poor in England had very few, if any, opportunities to better themselves. Coming to America gave them freedom from that oppressive economic system.

By the eighteenth century, people started to come to America to find new opportunities rather than just to escape English policies, so relations between the colonists and the British were generally friendly. However, this relationship began to deteriorate in 1763. The British had spent a lot of money to fight

Most of the first colonists were Puritans, a group of radical Christians who had broken away from English Protestantism. They left England because they didn't agree with ideas in the Church of England or with Elizabeth I. This is an artist's rendering of Puritans, or Pilgrims, going to church.

the French and Indian War, and when it ended they were left with a lot of debt. In order to pay this debt, the British raised taxes throughout the country and its colonies without the consent of the colonists. The unrest this created led to the American Revolution.

TAXATION WITHOUT REPRESENTATION

Today, citizens of the United States can vote to try to change laws or politicians they don't like, but before the American Revolution, colonists had very little say in British government. The only people whose votes mattered were the king and members of British parliament, most of whom cared a lot more about the people that lived in Britain than the colonists. The colonists felt like they didn't have anyone to represent them in government. They had no legal way to argue or influence the laws passed across the Atlantic Ocean, so the colonists were forced to live with whatever laws Parliament passed. The idea "Taxation without Representation" became very important during the Revolutionary War, as it highlighted the colonists' anger at having to pay taxes when they had no one to represent them in Parliament.

The Bill of Rights

SUSPICIOUS SEARCHES

To help pay debts from the French and Indian War, Britain raised taxes on the colonists. The taxes created by the Sugar Act and the Currency Act, both passed in 1764, caused a significant economic depression in the colonies, creating a climate of unrest and anger among the American colonists. The Stamp

Act of 1765 contributed even further to the colonists' anger. It imposed a tax on all printed documents and the colonists were forced to purchase official stamps before they could issue any written works, including newspapers, books, legal documents, and even marriage licenses.

To the colonists, British enforcement of the Stamp Act was as frustrating as the tax itself. Parliament issued legal papers called "writs of assistance" to British customs inspectors in order to enforce the collection of taxes. These writs gave inspectors the right to forcibly search the home or workplace of any colonist in order to find evidence of tax evasion, even if they had no evidence that the colonist was guilty. American colonists effectively had no privacy, even in their own homes. It was anger over these kinds of searches that led the Founding Fathers to include the Fourth Amendment in the Bill of Rights when they were forming their new government.

Taxation didn't stop with the Stamp Act. The Townshend Acts (1767) and the Tea Act (1773) created more taxes that further angered the colonists. They decided to officially notify Britain of their anger, and delegates from each colony attended a meeting later called the First Continental Congress. One of the principal achievements of the Congress was the drafting and ratification of a declaration of personal rights. This declaration was a forerunner to the Bill of Rights. It guaranteed the colonialists the rights to life, liberty, property, assembly, and trial by jury.

Members of the Second Continental Congress meet in May 1775 to make decisions about how to direct the war effort that had begun in April 1775 with the Battles of Lexington and Concord.

CREATING THE CONSTITUTION

The delegates of the First Continental Congress also put together several lists of grievances. They denounced England's policy of taxation without representation as well as the presence of the British army in the colonies without the consent of the colonists. In 1775, the colonists sent their grievances to the king of England, but King George III didn't seem to care. The British military was large and powerful, and the king would use it to enforce British law in the colonies whether the colonists liked it or not. The colonists grew angrier and angrier, and finally decided they had to use violence. In April 1775, the first shots of the American Revolution were fired in Lexington, Massachusetts.

The American War of Independence was long and arduous, but it finally ended in 1783. At that time the thirteen colonies were united under an agreement called the Articles of Confederation. The articles were America's first attempt to govern itself as an independent nation.

The Articles of Confederation provided the first basic framework for the government of the newly created United States. They fell short, however, in establishing a strong central government. At first, the Founding Fathers thought this was a good thing, but they soon found that a strong central government was necessary to enforce laws and unite the states into a single nation. In 1788, on the recommendation of Alexander Hamilton, delegates from each state met in Philadelphia to work together try to create a better government. It was at this meeting that the Constitution of the United States was written.

PROTECTING THE RIGHTS OF THE PEOPLE

In 1788, the Constitution of the United States was written and ratified. The Constitution is a brilliant and far-reaching document that delineates the powers of the federal and the state governments with a system of checks and balances, so that no one branch of government is more powerful than another.

The Constitution is comprehensive in outlining the powers of the federal and state governments. However, shortly after its final draft was completed, George Mason, a delegate from the state of Virginia noted that it said nothing in regards to the rights of the people. Mason was very bothered by this omission. After all, only twelve years earlier the British government had violated the personal freedoms of the colonists through their taxation without representation and the searches done under the writs of assistance. Now, a new powerful government was being created. What guarantee did its citizens have that this government would not trample their rights as well?

Mason was not the only delegate who was alarmed by the omission of individual liberties from the Constitution. James Madison and Thomas Jefferson were equally concerned. Jefferson wanted to see provisions in the Constitution that guaranteed people freedom of religion, freedom of the press, and protection against standing armies.

By June 1788, nine states had ratified the Constitution. Technically only nine states needed to ratify it for it to become the law of the land, but the fact that Virginia and New York had not ratified the document caused a great deal of concern. Virginia and New York were large and powerful states, and without the support of these two states, many delegates felt that the Constitution would ultimately fail to hold the new nation together. In addition, five of the nine states that had ratified the Constitution did so on the condition that amendments ensuring human rights would be added immediately.

In September 1791, when the first Congress met in New York City, calls for amendments protecting individual rights were nearly unanimous. A few months earlier, at the urging of several states, James Madison had drawn up amendments that he felt addressed the concerns of the delegates. These amendments were

James Madison was the main author of the Constitution and the fourth president of the United States.

presented to Congress, and by December 1791, the ten amendments we know as the Bill of Rights were ratified.

CHAPTER TWO

BALANCING PRIVACY *with* PUBLIC SAFETY

The American Revolution freed colonists from British rule and allowed them to create their own government from scratch. The Founding Fathers looked to many models, including the democracies of Ancient Greece, to help them decide how to structure the American government, but many ideas in the Constitution and the Bill of Rights came out of American anger at the British. The colonists had revolted because they felt that British government had failed them, so they worked to create a government that would solve many of the problems they saw in the British model.

For example, the colonists had resented the writs of assistance, which allowed British officials to enter their homes at will to search for evidence of tax evasion.

The writs of assistance allowed British soldiers to enter the homes of American citizens without a warrant. In this woodcut from the 1700s, British soldiers, recognizable by their red coats, ransack a colonist's home.

The Founding Fathers wrote the Fourth Amendment so that nothing like that could ever happen again unless it absolutely had to. The idea of the Fourth Amendment itself— that a government should be limited in its power to intrude into a citizen's home—was not a new one. This premise had long been argued by British legal theorists, but such warrants had enjoyed a long history in England, predating the American colonies. Now that America was no longer confined to British laws and traditions, this idea could be put into legal practice with the Fourth Amendment and similar laws.

REASONABLE AND UNREASONABLE SEARCHES

From about 1290, Parliament gave royal officials nearly unlimited power to search persons, houses, and ships. These searches were done in an effort to collect customs taxes on products imported to and exported from Britain. In 1662, Parliament formalized the method for customs searches, and out of this formalization the writs of assistance were born. The writs gave customs officials the power to demand assistance from other officers, as well as bystanders, in their searches.

The Fourth Amendment protects people from "unreasonable" searches of their persons, houses, papers, and effects. This raises the question: What is a reasonable search? The text of the amendment itself does not offer a definition of either a "reasonable" or "unreasonable" search. For the most part judges and the Supreme Court have looked to the

Investigators with the Los Angeles County District Attorney's Bureau carry boxes out of a home that they searched after obtaining a warrant in April 2012.

next part of the amendment in helping them to determine what constitutes a reasonable search.

The Fourth Amendment specifies that "no Warrants shall be issued, but upon probable cause . . . and supported by Oath or affirmation." Built into the language of the amendment, then, is the requirement that a warrant be issued before a search is carried out. Without a warrant, a federal governmental search of an individual's house, person, papers, and effects is deemed to be unconstitutional.

BOYD v. UNITED STATES

The first major Supreme Court decision involving the Fourth Amendment came in the 1886 case *Boyd v. United States*. This case centered around E. A. Boyd, whose company had been contracted by the government to supply glass for several federal buildings in Philadelphia. Boyd offered to discount his finished glass to the government on the condition that the government would not make him pay duties on the raw glass that he imported for the job. Over time, the government began to suspect that Boyd was actually importing more duty-free glass than was needed for the government contract, thus getting duty-free glass to use for other jobs, which was illegal.

The government took Boyd to court, demanding that he give up the lucrative contract. Once in court, the trial judge demanded that Boyd present each and every invoice for the glass he had imported. At first Boyd resisted the judge's

OBTAINING A WARRANT

The need for a warrant to be obtained before an officer of the law can conduct a search is a crucial element of the Fourth Amendment. It is based upon the principle that law enforcement officers need to have their powers checked in some way. In order for a law officer to justify a request for a search warrant, that official must convince a neutral magistrate, usually a judge, that there is probable cause for the warrant to be issued. Evidence for probable cause must be supported by facts, not just suspicion. Once probable cause has been presented and affirmed, an official must also describe to a magistrate what crime has been committed and where specifically the search will be conducted. The Founding Fathers detested the idea of any sort of general warrants, such as the writs of assistance. It was important to them that warrants be of a specific nature in order to protect the rights of the individual.

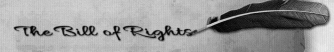

The Bill of Rights

order, but eventually he gave in and handed over all of his invoices. Based upon this evidence he was convicted.

Boyd was unhappy that he had been forced to hand over his invoices in court. He went on to appeal the decision to the Supreme Court. He appealed on the basis of his Fourth Amendment right of freedom from unreasonable searches and seizures and his Fifth Amendment right against self-incrimination.

The Supreme Court carefully considered whether Boyd's Fourth and Fifth amendment rights had been violated. They determined that by ordering Boyd to produce his invoices, the trial judge had indeed violated his rights under both amendments. They ruled that the right to be "secure" in one's person or dwelling means that a person should never be required to give up evidence that might be self-incriminating. The Court went on to order that a new trial take place, this time without the inclusion of Boyd's unconstitutionally acquired invoices as evidence.

Chief Justice Morrison Waite presided over the court that helped to protect E. A. Boyd's Fourth Amendment rights. He is pictured here in his robes, circa 1875.

THE EXCLUSIONARY RULE

While the Supreme Court's decision to hold a new trial in the *Boyd* case worked, it was not practical for the court system to have trials repeated. The expense and time would be too great to retry many cases in this manner. Based upon this, the Supreme Court created the exclusionary rule to deal with evidence that had been acquired in violation of the Fourth Amendment.

The Supreme Court first used the exclusionary rule in the 1914 case *Weeks v. United States*. The *Weeks* case involved the arrest of Fremont Weeks and the warrantless search of his home. Weeks was convicted based upon the ill-gotten evidence. He went on to appeal the conviction to the Supreme Court based upon his Fourth Amendment rights.

The Court overturned Weeks's conviction. In the process, it adopted the new policy that any evidence that was seized in violation of the Fourth Amendment was to be excluded from trial. This policy became known as the exclusionary rule because evidence is *excluded* from the trial if the collection of such evidence violates the defendant's constitutional rights.

CHAPTER THREE

THE FOURTH AMENDMENT *in the* SUPREME COURT

We usually think of the Constitution and its amendments as all-powerful mechanisms of protection, but it's important to remember that as it is written, the Bill of Rights only applied to the federal government. Unless the Supreme Court or another law said otherwise, state governments, private institutions, and other people had no obligation to respect a person's constitutional rights. Today, individual people and private companies still don't have to respect anyone's constitutional rights, but state governments do, thanks to the Fourteenth Amendment.

The Fourteenth Amendment did many things, including establishing who counts as a citizen of the United States. In relation to the Bill of Rights, it extended the protections of federal law to all citizens in all states. Since all U.S. citizens were entitled to the protections of the Bill of Rights in federal matters, the Fourteenth Amendment theoretically extended those protections to state actions. These protections were painfully slow in arriving, however, as conservative Supreme Court justices limited the extension of the guarantees provided by the Bill of Rights.

CHIEF JUSTICE EARL WARREN: PROTECTING THE RIGHTS OF ALL INDIVIDUALS

When Earl Warren accepted the position of chief justice of the Supreme Court in 1953, he faced the challenge of dealing with a deeply divided Court. Some of the justices felt strongly that the Court should have a more active role in the application of justice, while other justices favored the path of judicial restraint.

Warren proved to be very effective in building consensus among the justices. The history-making case *Brown v. Board of Education* (1954) was one of the first that Warren had to deal with as chief justice. In this case, the Court overturned the long controversial "separate but equal" doctrine, thus opening the path for the racial integration of America's public schools.

The Warren Court staunchly defended the individual rights of Americans. Warren considered it the job of the Court to prohibit the government from acting unfairly against the individual. Between 1961 and 1969, the Warren Court accomplished what previous Courts had

Earl Warren was the Chief Justice of the United States Supreme Court from 1953 to 1969. He is pictured here in his judge's robes.

resisted: it applied the procedural guarantees of the Bill of Rights to the states' administration of criminal justice.

In the rulings of cases such as *Mapp v. Ohio* (1961), which extended the exclusionary rule to the states, and *Miranda v. Arizona* (1966), which ensured that the police read a suspect his or her rights before any questioning could occur, Warren established the Court as the ultimate protector of civil rights and civil liberties.

CHIEF JUSTICE WARREN EARL BURGER: WORKING TOWARD THE GREATER GOOD

The Supreme Court of the 1970s and 1980s, led by Chief Justice Warren Earl Burger, tended to interpret the Bill of Rights in a different manner than the Warren Court. Crime was on the rise in America in the 1970s. The Supreme Court felt strongly that it needed to protect the safety of the general public, even if it meant interpreting the Bill of Rights in a way that put a higher priority on the safety of the public than on the rights of the individual.

Among other things, the Burger Court lowered the requirements for what they felt constituted a valid police search. The Court ruled in the 1971 *United States v. Harris* ruling that a suspect's reputation alone was sufficient to seek a search warrant. The Burger Court also made a number of exceptions to the exclusionary rule that the Warren Court had previously imposed upon the states. In 1984, the Court made two important exceptions to the rule:

In the *United States v. Leon* case, a warrant had been issued by a judicial officer to search the homes and cars of various people suspected of drug-related criminal activity. The suspects were convicted based upon the evidence discovered. The warrant, however, was issued based on dated information from an informant whose reliability was questionable.

This photo, taken in April 1972, is of Chief Justice Warren Burger, who led the Supreme Court from 1969 to 1986.

A federal court of appeals subsequently overturned the conviction, based upon the premise that the information used to obtain the warrant did not support probable cause. However, the Court overruled the decision of the appeals court and declared that the search was indeed valid. They believed the police were acting in "good faith" and therefore the search should be considered legal. By "good faith" the Court meant that the police had followed procedure and had taken time to present their case to get a warrant. The Court ruled that as long as the police were acting in good faith, the evidence should be admissible, even if the warrant itself was not valid.

The other key exception that the Court granted in 1984 to the exclusionary rule was termed "inevitable discovery." Inevitable discovery means that, as long as the prosecution can demonstrate that legally gathered evidence would have eventually led to the discovery of any illegally seized evidence, the illegally seized evidence can still be used in court.

CHIEF JUSTICE WILLIAM REHNQUIST: FAITH IN THE "GOOD FAITH RULE"

By 1980, the crime rate in the Unites States remained uncomfortably high. A 1982 report issued by the Attorney General's Task Force on Violent Crime stated that the costs to society of the exclusionary rule were unacceptably high, because it allowed too many criminals to go free. Numerous attempts were made during President Ronald Reagan's first administration to further restrict or abandon the exclusionary rule altogether. It was in this environment that William Rehnquist was appointed chief justice.

Rehnquist had been dissatisfied with the Warren Court's ruling in *Mapp v. Ohio*, and he vehemently opposed the exclusionary rule. He felt that excluding relevant evidence from an illegal search hampered the police in their ability to administer justice. He was less concerned that the police might conduct illegal searches than he was that criminals might be allowed to get away with illegal activities.

Following Warren Burger, William Rehnquist was the Chief Justice of the Supreme Court. Here he is posing in his chamber the day he became Chief Justice.

The Rehnquist Court first addressed the exclusionary rule in the 1987 case *Illinois v. Krull*. In this case police had relied upon a state law, which was later declared unconstitutional, to authorize a search. The Court decided to extend the good faith rule in this case and allowed the evidence to stand. In a later case, *Arizona v. Evans* (1995), the Rehnquist Court

"REASONABLE" SEARCHES OF STUDENTS

There have been a few important Supreme Court cases that have revolved around the Fourth Amendment protections that students should enjoy at schools. In one important case, *New Jersey v. T.L.O.* (1984), the Court ruled that the Fourth Amendment did indeed apply to the public school system. The Court went on to explain, however, that in the search process, school officials should not be held to the same standards as law enforcement. Instead, school officials should be held to a more general standard of whether a search is "reasonable under the circumstances." This means that the search must be performed only if the official expects to turn up evidence that a student has violated school rules. The Court also requires that the search not be unnecessarily intrusive. In the 1995 decision of *Vernonia School District v. Acton*, the Court stated that, while a child has an expectation of privacy, this expectation is less than what an adult enjoys. This language grants school officials leeway in deciding what types of searches are "reasonable" when it comes to students.

The Bill of Rights

extended the good faith rule yet again. In this case, the Court found that even though a warrant was issued in error, based upon a mistake in an official database, the evidence should still be admissible.

SEARCHES NOT NEEDING A WARRANT

There are some kinds of searches that have can be undertaken without a warrant in order to protect the public. Determining which type of search is "reasonable" however, has not been without controversy.

• Searches Performed with Consent

If an officer asks permission to search a suspect's home and the suspect gives permission to do so, the search is considered constitutional and any and all evidence discovered in the search is allowable in court. The suspect, by allowing the search, has essentially waived his or her Fourth Amendment rights.

• Searches Performed by Private Citizens

The Fourth Amendment does not cover searches performed by a private citizen, only governmental searches. A person's employer, for example, may search an employee's desk or other work areas without violating the Fourth Amendment in any way whatsoever.

• Searches Involving Evidence in Plain View

Police may seize any evidence not specifically covered by a warrant as long as they are lawfully in the area to begin with and the evidence is in plain view. For example, if the police have a warrant to search for a gun used in a robbery, and they see the actual stolen goods lying around, they can seize these goods even though they are not mentioned in the warrant. This also applies if the police actually witness an illegal activity. For example, if the police witness a man doing illegal drugs in public they may search him and arrest him.

• Frisking of Suspicious Individuals

Frisking refers to the practice of a police officer "patting down" a person who is suspected of having committed or is on his or her way to committing a crime. Originally, frisking

Protestors, led by Reverend Al Sharpton, obstruct twenty New York City blocks in a protest against Stop and Frisk.

only applied to searching for weapons, but in 1993, the Court expanded this type of search to include the confiscation of any sort of illegal items, such as drugs.

Stop-and-frisk is a program in New York City that allows police to stop anyone they believe looks suspicious and frisk them for illegal items. Many people allege that police often exhibit major racial biases in terms of the people they choose to stop, and this makes the program very controversial.

• Arrests of Suspects

During an arrest, the police have the right to search a person and the area around him or her without a warrant. There are three main reasons for this, all of which the Supreme Court has decided are in the public interest:

1. The suspect might be concealing weapons.
2. To prevent the escape of the suspect.
3. To prevent the destruction of any evidence at a crime scene.

CHAPTER FOUR

THE PROBLEM *of* NEW TECHNOLOGY

At heart, the Fourth Amendment is about preserving Americans' privacy. "The right of the people to be secure in their persons, houses, papers, and effects, against unreasonable searches and seizures, shall not be violated, and no Warrants shall issue, but upon probable cause, supported by Oath or affirmation, and particularly describing the place to be searched, and the persons or things to be seized." In other words, if a person has done nothing wrong, they should be able to keep their bodies, homes, papers, and other belongings private. But privacy must be balanced with public safety: sometimes, governments have to invade citizens' privacy in order to keep them safe.

But the meaning of "privacy" has changed a lot since the Fourth Amendment was ratified in 1791.

Back then, there was no way that the Founding Fathers could imagine all of the new technology that the government could someday put to use in collecting information in criminal investigations. In order to figure out what kinds of technology the Fourth Amendment should protect, the Supreme Court has passed judgment on a number of cases that involve technology, particularly when it comes to electronic surveillance.

WATCHING AND LISTENING FROM AFAR

In 1928, the Court heard the case *Olmstead v. United States*. The *Olmstead* case centered on the use of wiretaps by federal agents to listen to phone calls made and received by Roy Olmstead, a man suspected of illegally brewing homemade liquor. *Olmstead* is an especially notable case because it was the first Supreme Court ruling involving electronic surveillance of any kind.

Without the use of a search warrant, federal agents placed wiretaps in the basement of Olmstead's building (where he maintained an office) and in areas outside his home. Olmstead was subsequently convicted based on information gathered from the wiretaps. When the case was appealed to the Supreme Court, the Court had to decide whether wiretapping was covered by the protections of the Fourth Amendment.

The Court came to the conclusion that the wiretapping that had occurred in the investigation was not a violation of Olmstead's Fourth Amendment rights because the agents

Justice Louis Brandeis, for whom Brandeis University is named, served on the Supreme Court from 1916-1939.

had not actually entered into Olmstead's home or office to perform the wiretaps. The Court held that unless it involved an illegal entry into a home or office, the use of wiretapping was not prohibited by the Constitution.

Justice Louis Brandeis argued against the majority decision, arguing that the Fourth Amendment was meant to individual privacy as well as the physical invasion of the home. Brandeis wrote, "The progress of science, in furnishing the Government with means of espionage is not likely to stop with wiretapping." Brandeis thought that new technologies would likely make physical invasions obsolete, and therefore that the Supreme Court should work to protect the *purpose* of the Fourth Amendment, not its literal interpretation. He believed upholding the spirit of the law was key to making it useful for future generations.

In 1934, Congress passed a law that made it illegal to intercept the private communications of another and to reveal any of the gathered information, thus aligning itself

DRUG TESTING AT WORK AND IN SCHOOL

The Supreme Court has classified drug tests, whether by breath, blood, or urine, as searches as protected under the Fourth Amendment. Therefore, anyone performing a drug test must have a good reason to do so. Public health and safety is considered one of these reasons. Thus in 1989, when President Reagan issued an executive order requiring employees of the U.S. Customs Service to undergo urinalysis drug testing, the Court allowed such a measure to stand, even though there was no reason to suspect workers of being under the influence of drugs. The danger and unlawfulness of being intoxicated in certain situations, like at work in the U.S. Customs Service, seems to fall under the umbrella of public safety. This type of testing without suspicion is very controversial. Many feel that it is an infringement upon personal freedom. In addition to allowing testing without suspicion for drugs in the workplace, the Court has also held that schools have the right to perform such testing. Such a ruling was passed down in 1995 in *Vernonia School District v. Acton*.

The Bill of Rights

with Brandeis's argument. The Court subsequently followed the law passed by Congress. In *Nardone v. United States* (1939), the Court's ruling made it clear that federal agents, and indeed anyone else, were forbidden to use wiretapping technology to intercept telephone calls.

EVOLVING TECHNOLOGY

Because of the rapid pace of technological innovation in modern America, maintaining the Fourth Amendment's protections for individuals is certainly not easy. The Court faces a massive task in determining the proper role that new technology can play in future government investigations.

In 2001, the Supreme Court of the United States heard the seminal Fourth Amendment case *Kyllo v. United States*, which revolved around the use of a new technology called thermal imaging. In 1992, Special Agent William Elliot used a thermal-imaging device to detect the level of heat within Danny Kyllo's home. Elliot suspected that Kyllo was growing marijuana in his home. Elliot knew that special lights were needed to grow marijuana indoors, and that these lights generated a great deal of heat. The thermal-imaging device showed that an unusually large amount of heat was being generated in Kyllo's house. With the help of this discovery, Elliot was able to secure a warrant from a judge to search Kyllo's home.

Upon conducting the search, law enforcement officers found a grow farm consisting of more than one hundred marijuana plants in Kyllo's home. Based upon this evidence,

Thermal cameras show concentrations of heat. The red parts of the image are warmer than the blue parts, with the yellow in between.

a grand jury indicted Kyllo for the crime of manufacturing marijuana. Kyllo argued that a warrant was required for the thermal imager to be used in the first place. The trial court denied Kyllo's motion, and he was subsequently convicted. Kyllo appealed, or petitioned against, the decision. A court of appeals heard the case three times before coming to the conclusion that the use of thermal imaging in this case was

A Transportation Security Administration (TSA) officer checks a scan for suspicious concentrations of metal or hard matter like plastic. The image in the background is from a full-body scanner.

not a violation of Kyllo's Fourth Amendment rights. Kyllo, unsatisfied with the ruling, made one final appeal to the Supreme Court.

In a 5-4 decision, the Supreme Court reversed the lower courts' previous rulings and declared that the targeting of a home by law officers with a thermal imager is in fact a search under the Fourth Amendment. The Court stated, "At the very core of the Fourth Amendment stands the right of a man to retreat into his own home and there be free from unreasonable governmental intrusion." Even though the law enforcement had not intruded on Kyllo's home, their use of thermal imaging—a new technology that let them, in a way, see into his building without entering was classified as a search by the Supreme Court.

Another new technology of note is the body-scanning technology that is being implemented in airports by the Transportation Security Administration (TSA). Such imaging technology has the ability to see directly through a person's clothes, essentially rendering him or her naked. The TSA asserts that the technology is needed in order to keep airline passengers safe from those who wish to bring weapons or explosives onto flights. Many advocates of individual rights see these searches as pushing, and possibly breaking, the boundaries of our Fourth Amendment rights.

CONCLUSION

When dealing with issues relating to our Fourth Amendment rights, the Supreme Court faces the monumental challenge of balancing the rights of the individual against the needs of the government to protect national security. Since the terrorist attacks of September 11, 2001, issues of national security have risen to levels of the utmost importance. Yet the Supreme Court must uphold the Constitution of the United States, including protecting citizens according to the individual freedoms outlined in the Bill of Rights regardless of the national security climate.

Two challenges to Fourth Amendment protections since September 11 have come in the form of the USA PATRIOT Act and Homeland Security Act, which were passed shortly after the 2001 terrorist attacks. Both of these acts expanded the power of the federal government.

Some of the more controversial aspects of the acts are:

- Expanding the government's ability to look at records of an individual's activity being held by third parties. This means, for example, that the government can monitor an individual's internet history or emails without their knowledge.

President George W. Bush discusses the PATRIOT Act on April 19, 2004.

- Expanding the government's ability to search private property without notice to the owner. Such secret searches represent an obvious threat to established Fourth Amendment protections.
- "Trap and trace searches," which expand another Fourth Amendment exception for spying in order to collect information about the origin and destination of certain communications even if the communications themselves are left unread.

41

The task of the Supreme Court is to figure out how exactly to balance the rights of the individual with the needs of the country. Their decisions will make a big difference when challenges to the provisions of these new acts eventually find their way to the Court. Indeed, some of the acts' provisions have already been struck down by lower courts as violations of the Fourth Amendment. Many proponents of individual rights have objected to this expansion of governmental power, as they feel that it impinges upon civil liberties. Others believe that civil liberties should not matter because too much is at stake.

THE BILL OF RIGHTS

First Amendment (proposed 1789; ratified 1791): Freedom of religion, speech, press, assembly, and petition

Second Amendment (proposed 1789; ratified 1791): Right to bear arms

Third Amendment (proposed 1789; ratified 1791): No quartering of soldiers in private houses in times of peace

Fourth Amendment (proposed 1789; ratified 1791): Interdiction of unreasonable search and seizure; requirement of search warrants

Fifth Amendment (proposed 1789; ratified 1791): Indictments; due process; self-incrimination; double jeopardy; eminent domain

Sixth Amendment (proposed 1789; ratified 1791): Right to a fair and speedy public trial; notice of accusations; confronting one's accuser; subpoenas; right to counsel

Seventh Amendment (proposed 1789; ratified 1791): Right to a trial by jury in civil cases

Eighth Amendment (proposed 1789; ratified 1791): No excessive bail and fines; no cruel or unusual punishment

Ninth Amendment (proposed 1789; ratified 1791): Protection of unenumerated rights (rights inferred from other legal rights but that are not themselves coded or enumerated in written constitution and laws)

Tenth Amendment (proposed 1789; ratified 1791): Limits the power of the federal government

New American. "TSA and the Fourth Amendment: Take Another Look." Retrieved April 1, 2010. http://www.thenewamerican. com/index.php/usnews/constitution/3091-tsa-and-the-fourth-amendment-take-another-look.

Ramen, Fred. *The Right to Freedom from Searches*. New York, NY: Rosen Publishing, 2001.

"SCOTUSblog: Supreme Court of the United States Blog." Retrieved November 1, 2016. http://www.scotusblog.com.

Smith, Rich. *Fourth Amendment: The Right to Privacy*. Edina, MN: ABDO Publishing Company, 2008.

Street Law, Inc., and the Supreme Court Historical Society. "Landmark Supreme Court Cases." Retrieved April 1, 2010. http://www.landmarkcases.org.

Glossary

appeal To ask a higher court to reverse the decision of a lower court.

controversy A dispute or argument between sides holding opposing views.

conviction The act or process of finding or proving someone guilty.

defendant A person who has been accused of committing a crime.

delegate A person chosen to speak, act, or otherwise represent others.

effects A person's personal belongings.

enforce To make something happen by force.

evasion Escaping or avoiding something.

evidence Facts or signs that help one to find out the truth or come to a conclusion.

exclusion To leave something out.

magistrate A local law official, such as the judge of a police court.

obtain To gain or get by means of planning or effort.

omission Something that is left out.

overrule To reject or decide against.

parliament A legislature of a nation such as Canada or Great Britain.

possession The condition of having or owning something.

probable cause A reliable reason to believe that something may be true; in law, the grounds for suspicion for making a search.

ratify To make something legal by official approval.

rebellion Open, organized opposition toward an organization or entity, such as a government.

search warrant An official document that authorizes a search.

seizure The act of taking something by force.

suspect Someone who is thought to have committed a crime.

violate To disrespect or disobey something.

Further Reading

BOOKS

Krull, Kathleen and Anna DiVito. *A Kids' Guide to America's Bill of Rights*. Revised edition. New York, NY: HarperCollins, 2015.

Medina, Matthew J. *Real World Search & Seizure*. 2nd edition. Flushing, NY: Looseleaf Law Publications, 2012.

Quirk, Anne and Elizabeth Baddeley. *The Good Fight: The Feuds of the Founding Fathers (and How They Shaped the Nation)*. New York, NY: Knopf Books for Young Readers, 2017.

Rodgers, Kelly and Lynette Ordonez. *The New England Colonies: A Place for Puritans*. Huntington Beach, CA: Teacher Created Materials, 2016.

Thompson, Ben. *Guts & Glory: The American Revolution*. New York, NY: Little, Brown Books for Young Readers, 2017.

WEB SITES

Bill of Rights Institute
www.billofrightsinstitute.org

The Bill of Rights Institute sponsors programs to educate students about the ideas of the Founding Fathers and our basic freedoms.

Crime Museum
http://www.crimemuseum.org

This massive museum includes over one hundred interactive exhibits and artifacts pertaining to America's history of crime prevention and law enforcement.

The National Archives Experience
http://www.archives.gov

The public vaults at the archives hold over one thousand records, from presidential audio recordings and historic maps and photographs to facsimiles of important documents

Bibliography

American Civil Liberties Union. "Surveillance Under the USA/PATRIOT Act." Retrieved November 1, 2016. http://www.aclu.org/technology-and-liberty/surveillance-under-usapatriot-act.

Bodenhamer, David J., and James W. Ely Jr., eds. *The Bill of Rights in Modern America*. Bloomington, IN: Indiana University Press, 2008.

Cornell University Law School. "Kyllo v. The United States." Retrieved November 1, 2016. http://www.law.cornell.edu/supct/html/99-8508.ZS.html.

Dudley, William, ed. *The Bill of Rights: Opposing Viewpoints*. San Diego, CA: Greenhaven Press, 1994.

Head, Tom, ed. *The Bill of Rights* (Interpreting Primary Documents). San Diego, CA: Greenhaven Press, 2004.

Konvitz, Milton R. *Fundamental Rights: History of a Constitutional Doctrine*. New Brunswick, NJ: Transaction Publishers, 2001.

McInnis, Thomas N. *The Evolution of the Fourth Amendment*. Lanham, MD: Lexington Books, 2009.

Meserve, Jeanne, and Mike M. Ahlers. "Full Body Scanners Improve Security, TSA Says." Retrieved November 1, 2016. http://www.cnn.com/2010/TRAVEL/04/01/airport.body.scanners/index.html.

National Archives. "The Charters of Freedom: A New World Is at Hand." Retrieved November 1, 2016. http://www.archives.gov/exhibits/charters/bill_of_rights.html.

Index

A

American Revolution, 7, 11, 14
Articles of Confederation, 11

B

Bill of Rights, 5, 9, 13, 14, 22,
   23, 24, 32, 40
body scanning, 39
Brandeis, Louis, 34, 36
Burger Court, 24, 25
Burger, Warren Earl, 24

C

Constitution, 4, 11, 12, 13, 14,
   22, 34, 40

D

drug testing, 35

E

exclusionary rule, 20, 21, 24, 25,
   26, 27

F

Fifth Amendment, 20
Fourteenth Amendment, 22, 23
Fourth Amendment, 17, 28, 35,
   39, 40, 41, 42
     privacy, 5, 9, 28, 32, 34
     reasonable search, 16, 18, 28

unreasonable search, 4, 5,
   16, 19, 32
violation, 4, 5, 21, 33, 38, 42
warrants, 4, 16, 18, 19, 21,
   25, 26, 29, 30, 31, 32, 33,
   36, 37

R

Rehnquist Court, 27
Rehnquist, William, 26, 27

S

searches, 8, 9, 12, 16, 19, 27, 28,
   35, 39, 41
     arrests, 31
     by private citizens, 29
     evidence, 29–30
     frisking, 30–31
     with consent, 29
seizure, 4, 20, 32

T

thermal imaging, 36, 37, 38, 39

W

Warren Court, 23, 24, 25, 27
Warren, Earl, 23
wiretaps, 33–34, 36
writs of assistance, 9, 12, 14,
   16, 19